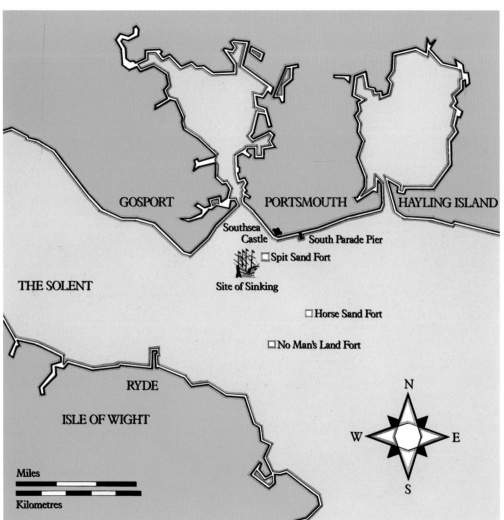

Map labels: GOSPORT · PORTSMOUTH · HAYLING ISLAND · Southsea Castle · South Parade Pier · Spit Sand Fort · Site of Sinking · THE SOLENT · Horse Sand Fort · No Man's Land Fort · RYDE · ISLE OF WIGHT · Miles · Kilometres · N · W · E · S

Contents

Acknowledgements

Cover and Page 2 by kind permission of The Pepys Library.
Page 21 background by permission of The British Library.
All other images The Mary Rose Trust.
Pages 14, 15, 17 Artist W. H. Bishop.
Page 16 left Photographer P. Langdown.
Text The Mary Rose Trust. ISBN 0 9511747 2 X

© **The Mary Rose Trust 9.2002.**   **Twelfth Impression.**

Floor Plan of the Museum

Please note that tickets are valid for both the Museum and Ship Hall.
We recommend that you visit the Museum before the Ship Hall.

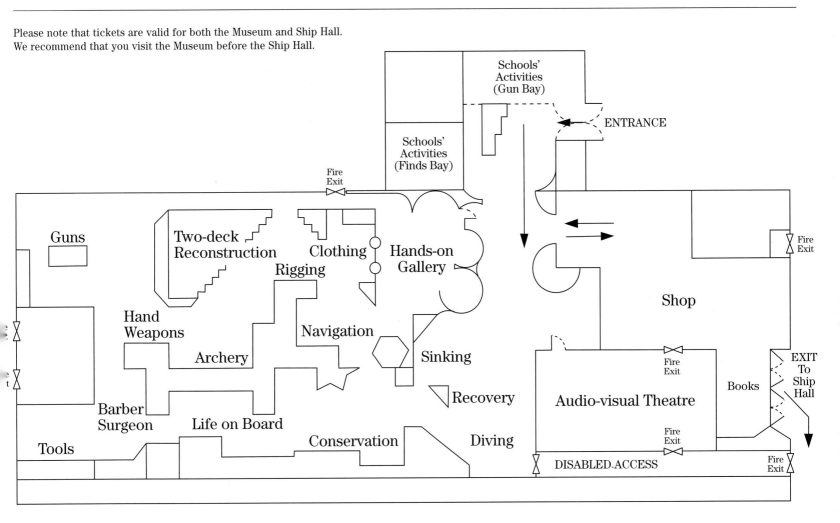

The Mary Rose Tunage Shipe

Tonnes of Brasse.   Tonnes of yron.   Gonnepowder   Shotte of yron   Shotte of Stoey and Leade

The only contemporary illustration of the *Mary Rose* comes from the Anthony Roll, a list of all King Henry VIII's vessels completed in 1546. The Roll records the name, tonnage and crew numbers of each vessel, together with an inventory of the weaponry and munitions carried on board.

Recent research and survey shows the *Mary Rose* to be somewhat different to the ship shown in this picture. (See page 14).

The Tudor Ship **Mary Rose**

Henry VIII inherited the nucleus of a royal fleet from his father, including such great ships as the *Regent* (1,000 tons) and the *Sovereign* (800 tons). However, faced with the ever-present threat of the French Navy as well as a strong, potentially hostile, Scottish fleet, he began an intensive programme of naval rearmament soon after he became King of England in 1509. Portsmouth became a hive of activity. The new King ordered the *Sovereign* to be rebuilt in the shipbuilding dock which had been constructed fourteen years earlier at a cost of £193 0s. 6¾d. and, no sooner was that job done, than the keels of two new ships were laid. The *Mary Rose* and the *Peter Pomegranate*.

The earliest reference to the ship by name, records payments made by the King in 1511 for the 'conveyance of our two new ships from Portsmouth unto the River Thames, the one of them called the *Mary Rose* the other called the *Peter Garnarde*'. Named after Henry's favourite sister, Mary, and his family emblem, the Tudor rose, the *Mary Rose* was a successful ship in the years following her launch, serving as the flagship of the English fleet. In a letter to the King, Admiral Sir Edward Howard described her as 'your good ship, the flower, I trow, of all ships that ever sailed'.

During the First French War (1512-1514) she took part in ferocious battles off the French port of Brest in 1512 and 1513, and an attack on towns and villages surrounding Cherbourg in 1514. While in 1513 she had sailed to Newcastle to fight against the Scots who had invaded England. In 1520 she served as escort to the King when he crossed the Channel to Calais to meet the French King, Francis I, at what was known as the Field of the Cloth of Gold. But diplomatic efforts at securing peace were short lived, and the next time she crossed the Channel was to wreak havoc during the Second French War (1522-1525). Despite the ever-present threat of war, particularly from Scotland in the North, the following years were a period of quiet for the *Mary Rose*, and it was during this time that the ship was refitted and uprated from her original 500 tons to 700 tons.

Then, in 1543, war with France broke out again, and in 1545, in response to the English capture of Boulogne, a French invasion fleet set sail for the South coast of England. The *Mary Rose*, under the command of Sir George Carew, was about to sail into her final battle.

It was on the 19th of July 1545, during the battle which saw the defeat of this fleet, that she sank. Though not as a result of French gunfire, what precisely happened to cause the disaster is unclear. But a possible explanation is as a result of mishandling and indiscipline amongst the crew.

One source, the Ambassador of the Holy Roman Emperor, Francis Van der Delft reported that 'one of the survivors, a Fleming, told me that the disaster was caused by their not having closed the lowest row of gun ports on one side. Having fired the guns on that side, the ship was turning, in order to fire from the other (port) side, when the wind caught her sails so strongly as to heel her over, and plunge her open gunports beneath the water, which flooded and sank her.' Another source states that many of the mariners on board were ships' masters in their own right, and would not take orders from one another. John Hooker, the contemporary biographer of Sir George Carew's younger brother Sir Peter, wrote 'He (Sir George) had in this ship a hundred mariners, the worst of them being able to be a master in the best ship within the realm, and these so maligned and disdained one the other, that refusing to do that which they should do, were careless to do that which they ought to do ...'. Certainly, the last recorded words of Sir George, yelled to his uncle Sir Gawain, that he 'had a sort of knaves whom he could not rule' indicates a problem in getting the crew to obey orders. Whatever the exact nature of the problem, Sir George Carew appears to have had great difficulty in controlling the *Mary Rose*, and in this circumstance it is likely that essential tasks would not have been properly carried out. However, as with many maritime disasters, it was probably a combination of factors, innocuous by themselves but lethal in the right combination, that caused the catastrophe.

After the battle, attempts were made to salvage the ship. Expert Venetian salvors were hired to undertake the work and, on the 1st of August, it was reported that 'by Monday or Tuesday the *Mary Rose* shall be weighed up and saved'. But such confidence was premature. Despite strenuous efforts she remained stuck fast on the sea-bed, and by December of 1545 the task had been abandoned.

Although some guns were recovered from the ship over the next four years, the *Mary Rose* gradually faded into obscurity. It would be over 400 years before she finally returned to Portsmouth.

1509-1511 Built in Portsmouth for King Henry VIII and listed as 400 tons. The ship now lies within a few hundred metres of where she was built. The bronze bell was recovered from the starboard side of the ship in 1982. It bears an inscription in Flemish dated 1510 and was probably made by Willem van den Ghein of Mechlin who cast bells for Iona Cathedral and Peterhouse, Cambridge.

1536 Rebuilt and uprated to 700 tons. Fitted with new cast bronze muzzle-loading guns including three which bear the date 1535. The inscription *Pour Defender*, on the demi cannon cast by Francesco Arcanus, reflects Henry VIII's defensive policy and his enthusiasm for the new guns being made for him in London.

1545 Sank during an engagement with a French invasion fleet two kilometres from the entrance to Portsmouth Harbour, in fourteen metres of water. Very few men survived the disaster.

1836 Pioneer divers, John and Charles Deane discovered the site of the wreck and recovered a bronze demi cannon gun probably made at a foundry at Salisbury Place, London by Archangelo de Arcanis in 1542. The gun fits on a collapsed carriage excavated by the archaeologists in 1981, on the main deck at the stern of the ship.

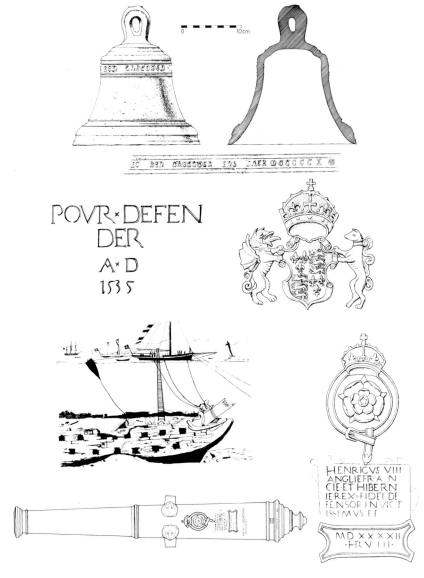

1965-1971 Led by Alexander McKee, divers searched for the ship on the sea-bed, eventually using side scan and sub-bottom sonar equipment. The Mary Rose (1967) Committee leased the area where the ship lay, and a programme of exploration and survey was started by volunteer divers, scientists and archaeologists.

1971-1979 Frames, planking and deck beams were seen, and a series of limited excavations outside the ship were carried out to determine how much survived. In 1978, a trench across the wreck at the bow confirmed that two decks survived *in situ* at this point. It was decided that the ship should be totally excavated and recorded. The Mary Rose Trust was formed in 1979 with H.R.H. Prince Charles as president. Full-time staff were appointed to carry out the work of excavating the ship and her contents. Over 600 volunteer divers, and many more volunteers on shore, helped with the work.

1979-1982 The ship was excavated, recorded and prepared for recovery. Decks, cabins, bulkheads and companionways were surveyed, and brought ashore timber by timber. In total over 25,000 registered finds were brought ashore.

1982 The world witnessed the raising of the *Mary Rose* on 11th October 1982. Work continues to preserve the ship and her 'treasures', while making them available for the education and pleasure of the public.

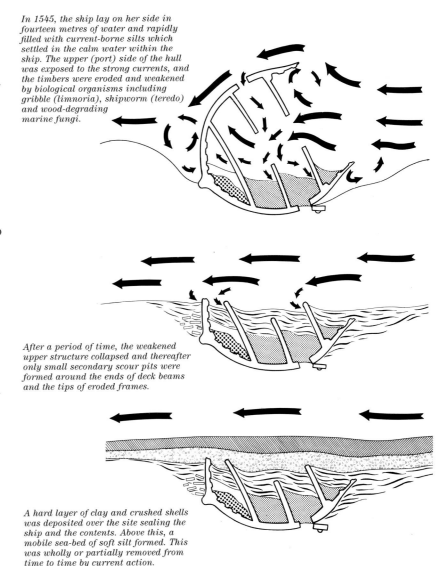

In 1545, the ship lay on her side in fourteen metres of water and rapidly filled with current-borne silts which settled in the calm water within the ship. The upper (port) side of the hull was exposed to the strong currents, and the timbers were eroded and weakened by biological organisms including gribble (limnoria), shipworm (teredo) and wood-degrading marine fungi.

After a period of time, the weakened upper structure collapsed and thereafter only small secondary scour pits were formed around the ends of deck beams and the tips of eroded frames.

A hard layer of clay and crushed shells was deposited over the site sealing the ship and the contents. Above this, a mobile sea-bed of soft silt formed. This was wholly or partially removed from time to time by current action.

Salvage and Recovery

January 1982

The Mary Rose Trust approved a plan to recover the remains of the hull in one piece in suspension from a purpose-designed lifting frame which would be attached to steel bolts passing through the hull at carefully selected points.

15th June 1982

A tubular steel lifting frame was placed in position and supported on four legs above the empty wreck. Lifting wires were attached to steel bolts which passed through the hull to backing plates on the outside. As each wire was firmly secured to a transom of the lifting frame, tunnelling could safely proceed beneath the hull to secure further lifting bolts and their backing plates.

28th September 1982

A steel cradle, lined with air bags and designed to conform to the shape of the hull, was placed on the sea-bed to the west of the wreck.

30th September/1st October 1982

With the wires in position and tensioned, the lifting frame was raised up the shafts of the legs using hydraulic jacks. Once the *Mary Rose* was above the sea-bed, the hull hung in suspension from the lifting frame.

9th October 1982

When tide and weather were suitable, the lifting frame was raised by the crane Tog Mor, and the hull, hanging in suspension from the frame, was moved underwater until it was over the cradle.

11th October 1982

Once the hull was safely in the cradle, the cradle was secured to the crane hook by lifting strops and the whole package, weighing 570 tonnes, was lifted into air and placed on the deck of a barge ready to be towed ashore.

The hull was now supported in the cradle on the barge and the lifting frame was obsolete, but it was impossible to remove it because of rapidly deteriorating weather and the whole 'package' was taken into Portsmouth Harbour to the safe haven of the Royal Naval Base.

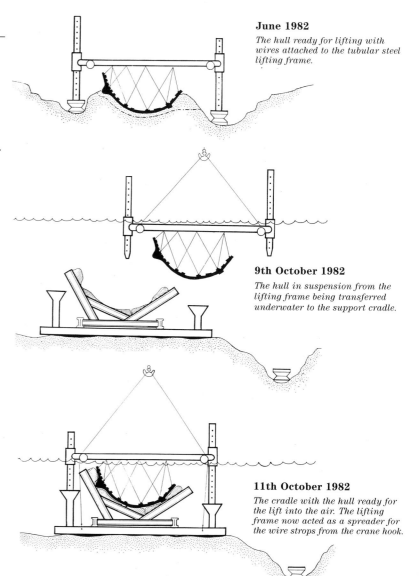

June 1982
The hull ready for lifting with wires attached to the tubular steel lifting frame.

9th October 1982
The hull in suspension from the lifting frame being transferred underwater to the support cradle.

11th October 1982
The cradle with the hull ready for the lift into the air. The lifting frame now acted as a spreader for the wire strops from the crane hook.

The hull of the Mary Rose was lifted in the support cradle inclined at sixty degrees from the vertical, exactly as she had lain on the sea-bed for 437 years. She is still supported in the same cradle which was modified when the ship was turned upright in 1985.

The weather forecast was poor on the day of recovery, but by the time the threatened gales occurred, the barge, cradle and hull were safely moored inside the harbour.

The success of the recovery operation was largely dependent on an accurate archaeological survey of the hull underwater. This was used by the structural engineers to design the support cradle. New methods of survey were evolved which enabled the archaeologists to quantify inaccuracies and reject spurious measurements which unfortunately occur all too frequently when divers are working in tidal conditions with poor visibility.

7

The Hull in No. 3 Dry Dock

The hull is housed in No. 3 Dry Dock which was completed in 1799 and is itself a scheduled monument.

Two-thirds of the dock is covered with a double-skinned, thermally insulated roof which helps maintain a stable environment in which to hold the hull.

During the **Passive Holding** phase (1982-1994) the Ship Hall temperature was maintained below 5°C and the humidity at around 95%. The hull was sprayed with recycled chilled fresh water to prevent drying and to control levels of fungi and bacteria. Sprays could be turned off for a maximum of just four one hour periods each day. This allowed reconstruction work to take place, as well as archaeological research and regular checks on the condition of the timbers.

A programme of **scientific trials** was undertaken during this period. Various conservation treatments using *Mary Rose* timbers and different grades of Polyethylene Glycol (PEG) were looked at in these experiments. The results indicated which combination of PEG grades were best suited to treat the hull, and the results were put to use when Active Conservation began.

In 1984, it was decided to rotate the cradle and **turn the hull upright**. This work was completed in July 1985 by a two-stage turning process, which used hydraulic jacks to pull the cradle up an inclined plane for the first stage of the rotation, and then deployed a system of jacking towers along the port side of the ship to control the lowering of the port side. The hull timbers were carefully monitored throughout the operation, but there was no movement of the structure.

Since the recovery of the *Mary Rose* in 1982, archaeologists had continued the survey and recording of the hull. Now with the ship restored to the upright position, the programme of work to replace those timbers surveyed and dismantled underwater could begin.

Reinsertion of the beams, carlings, knees and deck planks gives increased longitudinal strength to the existing structure, and enables the visitor to appreciate the *Mary Rose* for the fighting platform she was.

Restoring the Hull

During the years 1971 to 1982, some 3,000 timbers were recovered from the wreck site. Each was given a unique identity number, and brought ashore for study and conservation in advance of the recovery of the empty hull in October 1982. However, the most important group of timbers were the 800 we found *in situ*.

Longest is a plank seven metres long, while the largest single element is the rudder which weighs 750 kilograms. Handling these timbers was much more difficult in air than underwater and two **cranes** were installed to help carry out the task of restoring the hull.

In the photograph opposite, the crane is being used to replace one of the planks from the orlop deck. With a capacity of 1000 kilograms, at a maximum reach of eleven metres, they could also carry two members of staff in a personnel basket.

Additional support for the structure is provided by vertical props and horizontal struts made of **titanium**. This is an ideal material, being light, strong and resistant to corrosion. We have not tried to disguise these supports, as they enable the visitor to differentiate between the original Tudor oak and modern materials.

The reinstatement, in December 1993, of the last timber in the initial restoration programme, marked the end of yet another phase in the history of the *Mary Rose*, and allowed the project to progress to Active Conservation.

Replacement of the compartment and partition structures will, in view of conservation and mechanical requirements, occur after the main section of the hull is conserved – finally restoring the ship to the condition in which she was found underwater.

Conservation of the Hull

Active Conservation of the hull began in 1994 when **Polyethylene Glycol** (PEG), a water soluble wax, was introduced into the spray system. First developed in the 1950s, PEG treatments have proved highly successful for stabilising waterlogged archaeological wood. The conservation of the *Mary Rose* is using two different grades of PEG in separate stages of the treatment programme.

A **first phase** treatment, using a 'low grade' PEG solution, is now complete. The relatively small molecules of this grade were able to pass through the wood structure, and penetrate deep in to the heart of the timbers. Here they replaced the water in the cell walls, which will keep the wood fibres swollen when the final drying process begins, dramatically reducing shrinkage.

The **second phase,** using a 'high grade' PEG solution, began in 2003. With far larger molecules, this grade will only penetrate the outer layer of timbers, where degraded cell wall material will allow it to pass through. Once drying of the hull commences, this solution will actually solidify in the outer layer, providing mechanical support to the fragile cell wall remnants. Because this high grade solution is more difficult to spray, an entirely new spray system has had to be constructed. It is anticipated that this second phase will be complete by 2008. However, only analysis of samples from the hull will tell us exactly when enough PEG has penetrated the timbers.

Periodically small core samples are taken from timbers. These are analysed using a Liquid Chromatograph, to see how much PEG has penetrated and how far. Samples are also examined under a Scanning Electron Microscope to check that the condition of timbers is stable.

On completion of the second phase, a **final drying phase** will begin. An important research programme is currently underway, using climatic test chambers, to identify the best temperature and humidity conditions to dry the hull. Exactly how long the drying will take will depend on these conditions, but we anticipate as much as four years. Both during and after the drying programme, conservators will need to work on the hull, removing excess PEG and monitoring any movement of the timbers.

At the end of this process, the hull will be displayed in an open museum environment for the first time.

1. A member of the conservation team taking a core sample using an increment borer.
2. A conservation scientist examing the surface of a timber sample.
3. A Scanning Electron Micrograph of a section of oak taken from a Main Deck Knee.

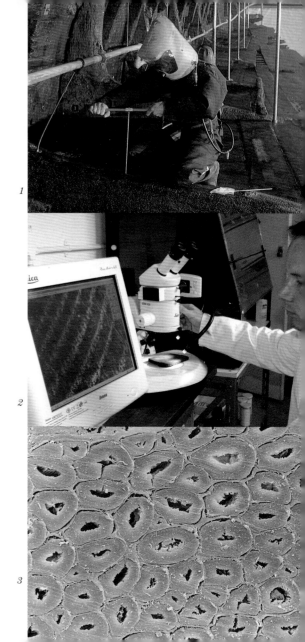

1

2

3

A member of the conservation team inspects main deck timbers at the stern of the ship. This is part of the routine inspection work that will continue throughout the conservation process.

Because of the fine mist and chemicals present in the spray, it is necessary for all members of the conservation team to wear full breathing apparatus while working in the Ship Hall. This allows up to forty-five minutes in which to take timber samples or replace blocked nozzles for example. The protective suits include a full radio-communication system which can be switched to a public address in the viewing gallery, allowing visitors to communicate with conservation staff whilst they are carrying out their work.

11

Conservation of Objects

Many objects of wood, leather, wool and silk were discovered in the sea-bed sealed in an anaerobic atmosphere beneath layers of fine silt. Once they were removed from this environment, distortion or collapse could occur quite rapidly if the objects were carelessly left to dry out. During the excavation, Finds Assistants worked on board the diving vessel *Sleipner* with the archaeologists, cataloguing and packing each object so that it could be safely taken ashore. Many objects were preserved by freeze drying; a process which involved 'bulking' the waterlogged object with an inert water soluble chemical such as polyethylene glycol (PEG), or manitol (a sugar alcohol) and then freezing it and then removing the water by sublimation under vacuum. Most of the wooden objects displayed in the museum were treated in this way.

All of the objects are displayed or stored in a closely controlled environment, as fluctuation in temperature or humidity can cause severe problems even after conservation.

We are now finding that better results can be obtained by treating waterlogged wood with low molecular weight PEG followed by PEG of higher molecular weight and ensuring that the penetration of the chemical is thoroughly achieved over a relatively long period of time. This method can be combined with freeze drying or used as a preliminary to controlled air drying.

Many metals objects were stabilised using reduction techniques. Wrought iron objects were heated in an atmosphere of hydrogen or reduced by electrolysis. Some of the pewter and bronze objects were subjected to intensive washing to remove free chlorides and were then solvent dried.

The Ship

Henry VIII's *Mary Rose* was one of the first of a new breed of purpose built warships. She was a successful fighting platform, far removed from the ill-equipped, under-gunned vessels of the previous century.

Until a way could be found to bring guns below decks it was impossible for ships to carry many large guns on board. The main problem seems to have been how to cut gun ports low in the hull and provide them with a watertight seal when the ship was underway in heavy seas. It was difficult to solve this problem as long as ships were clinker-built, that is with overlapping planks giving an uneven surface to the hull. But, with the development of smooth edge-to-edge carvel planking, shipbuilders were able to cut holes in the hull and, more importantly, fit them with efficient watertight lids.

The evidence contained within the hull suggests that the new style carvel planking was used from the outset and that, even at this time, the *Mary Rose* carried her heaviest guns on a purpose-built gun deck. What is also clear, is that claims of a design fault, in that the gun ports were too close to the water, are unsubstantiated by fact.

Built almost entirely of oak, no plans or drawings survive to show how she was originally designed, but it is inconceivable that the *Mary Rose* was built by 'rule of thumb'. Moreover, similarities between this ship and a mid-sixteenth-century Basque ship excavated in Red Bay, Labrador, Canada, suggest that there was a link between craftsmen building ships in Spain and those in England. The **keel** was made of three pieces, the fore and aft sections of elm and the midships section of oak, scarfed together to give a total length of thirty-two metres. Next the **stem and stern posts** were shaped and fastened to the keel with strong scarf joints. The **floor timbers** and then the **keelson** were laid over the keel and securely fastened with long iron bolts. Finally, the ends of the keel bolts were concealed and protected by wooden caps. **Riders** braced the bottom of the ship. These were cut to fit over or around the keelson and over the **stringers** which run fore and aft along the length of the ship and stiffen the hull. A series of **futtocks**, each cut and shaped to form the appropriate section of the **frames** or 'ribs' of the hull, were attached to the floor timbers and as this framework grew it was supported by timber shoring.

Within this framework **deck beams** were placed, running from side to side across the width of the ship. Held in position at their ends by **deck clamps** and **knees**, and supported at intervals across their length by **stanchions** or pillars, they braced the hull and formed part of the grid of timbers which supported the **decks**. Support for the decks was completed by a series of **carlings** and **half beams**. The carlings were set, running fore and aft, into the deck beams, while the half beams, running from side to side, were in turn rebated into the carlings. Once this network of timbers was in position the deck planks could then be laid in place and nailed down.

Between 1511 and 1545 the ship was modified several times, and considerably strengthened at some period with the addition of wooden **braces** which run diagonally from just below the waterline through the edge of the orlop deck and into the hold.

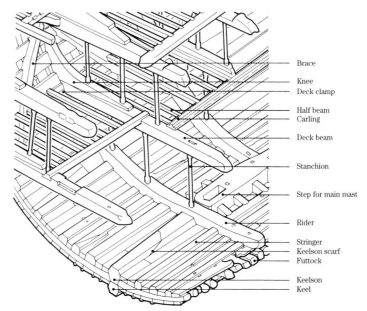

Brace
Knee
Deck clamp
Half beam
Carling
Deck beam
Stanchion
Step for main mast
Rider
Stringer
Keelson scarf
Futtock
Keelson
Keel

An impression of the **Mary Rose**

based on the evidence contained in the surviving structure of the hull

Guns were found *in situ* on the starboard side of the ship; seven on the main deck, three on the upper deck, four on the castle deck and one on the upper deck in the after castle (this gun fired forward from the after castle and it can be seen in the illustration opposite).

Armament

15 Heavy, cast bronze, muzzle loading guns
24 Heavy, wrought iron, breech loading guns
30 Wrought iron, breech loading swivel guns

Masts

Fore	Square rigged
Main	Square rigged
Mizzen	Lateen rigged
Bonaventure	Lateen rigged

Dimensions

Length	of keel	32 metres
	at waterline	38·5 metres
	stem to stern	40·9 metres
	total length	45 metres
Breadth		11·66 metres
Draught		4·6 metres
Height	of forecastle	12·2 metres
	of waist	10 metres
	of after castle	14 metres
Length	of forecastle	5·5 metres
	of waist	15 metres
	of after castle	20 metres

View of the starboard side of the after castle

The illustration (right) shows how the castle looked when it was excavated. The view is looking towards the stern, with the guns on the two decks exactly where they were found.

A strong shelf or **channel** ran the length of the hull beneath the after castle, and a similar channel ran below the forecastle. These served to spread the **chains** which connected to the **shrouds** which braced each of the four masts. Supported on sturdy brackets, similar brackets and standards rise from the channel to spread the load from the chains.

The main hull is carvel built with smooth edge-to-edge planking and the change to lighter 'clinker' planking occurs at the level of the upper deck gun port.

A wooden trough or **daile** protrudes through the hull below the channel. This served to carry away water brought up from the bilges by the **main pump** which was situated immediately aft of the main mast. A **second pump** was situated further astern close to the mizzen mast.

The stern portion of the starboard side, although rather obscured by the cradle, can be seen from the far end of the stern gallery.

Future plans include the provision of a viewing gallery on the north side of the dock. This view, and indeed the whole of the starboard side, will then be available to the visitor in comfort and safety.

Conservator restoring the only surviving sixteenth-century mast top in the world.

The small size of this top means it may have been intended for the junction of the main topmast and main topgallant, the third and highest section of the main mast. Given its size, it might have been purely decorative or possibly for use by a single lookout. It only survived Tudor salvage because it was in store below decks.

As well as some of the guns, the Venetian salvors did recover the masts and rigging. Because of this, the majority of the objects associated with the masts, found during the modern excavation of the ship, were spares stored in the forward part of the ship. The exception being parts of the standing rigging trapped beneath the after castle.

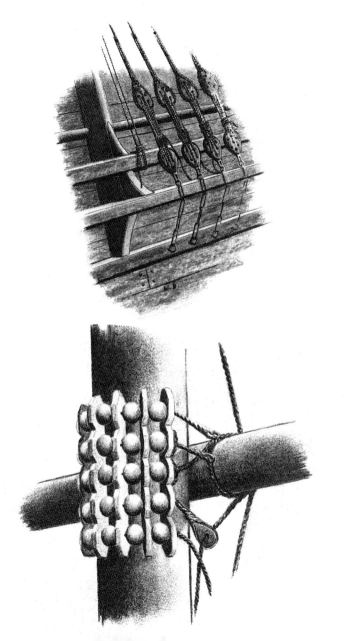

The Standing Rigging

This standing rigging was found *in situ* beneath the after castle (previous page, top right). The **channel** for the main, mizzen and bonaventure masts was a continuous 'platform like' structure which ran sternwards from the front of the after castle to the transom. The **channel, chains, deadeyes** and **lanyards** were extremely well preserved on the starboard side of the hull and they were recorded in detail during the excavation. The shroud from the standing rigging passed around (turned in) the upper of a pair of deadeyes, and was secured by 'throat seizing' just above the top of the deadeye and then at two further points.

The position of the two deadeyes relative to each other could be adjusted by a continuous lanyard, and the lower deadeye was bound with an iron band which was forged with an integral ring at the lower end. The chains were fastened to this ring and, at their lower end, to a ring bolt fastened to a wale immediately above the lower gun ports.

Parrels

A complete set of **parrel ribs** and **trucks**, still rigged and rolled into a neat bundle, was found in a store located in a forward compartment on the orlop deck (previous page, bottom right). When the bundle was unrolled it was found to be five rows of wooden trucks or balls interspersed by spacer ribs. Acting with a 'ball bearing' type of action they allowed the yard to be hoisted up the mast and secured in position. There was no trace of any block or thimble to connect the parrels to lifting tackle, or of the rope which must have run outside the ribs. Breast ropes or preventers were mentioned in inventories from the sixteenth century, and these may have been ropes which passed outside the parrels through the V-shaped notches to give greater security.

View from the Main Viewing Gallery towards the starboard side of the ship

☐ **Castle Deck:**
Guns

☐ **Upper Deck:**
Guns, cabin at stern, ready-to-use hand weapons

☐ **Main Deck:**
Guns, cabins (pilot, barber surgeon, carpenter's)

☐ **Orlop Deck:**
Stores, equipment, food, hand weapons

☐ **Hold:**
Ballast, galley, stores

This photograph was taken in 1993 before the upper deck was replaced.

1. Steel support cradle
2. Keel (elm)
3. Stern post
4. Seam covering battens
5. Oak carvel-built hull
6. Remains of iron pintle to which the rudder was attached
7. One of nine riders
8. Step for main mast in centre of the keelson
9. Frames (ribs) on the port side of the ship
10. One of six diagonal braces in the midship section
11. Deck carlings running fore and aft and supporting the half-beams. The half-beams and the deck planking were removed under water and put back into the ship before Active Conservation started
12. Rising knee
13. Gunnel or gunwale in the waist of ship. A screen of blinds light-weight boards of poplar, protected the archers and gunners above this point
14. One of seven gun ports on the main deck
15. One of three small openings for swivel guns cut through the clinker planking of the after castle on the upper deck
16. Forward end of after castle
17. Castle deck (the highest deck in the ship)
18. Maximum preserved height of ship
19. Frames (rib) high in the after castle on the starboard side of the ship
20. Bow section cut off forward of this point

STERN 19

Sailing and Navigation

Only a few years after the *Mary Rose* was built, Magellan completed the first circumnavigation of the world in ships provided by Charles I of Spain.

The ships he used were 'naos' – fully-rigged ships fitted with both square and lateen sails. Larger versions of the nao were carracks, very similar to the *Mary Rose*, which were able to sail effectively into the wind. They could thus use their square sails to venture downwind along an unfamiliar coast and still make their way safely back with the lateen sails.

These improvements in ship design, together with the development of the art of navigation, or the haven-finding art, at the end of the fifteenth century, made it possible to explore the world beyond Europe and North Africa and return home with precision and safety.

Tide tables and pilot's books, or rutters were used, containing written sailing instructions recording in detail the coastal landscape, prevailing winds, depth of water and nature of the sea-bed.

One of the three compasses from the Mary Rose.

The second-century geographer, Ptolemy, had developed a system of dividing the globe into 360 degrees and he devised a formula which described how the length of a degree longitude changed with latitude. Renaissance cartographers used and improved Ptolemy's maps and projections, and they formed a basis for mapping the new discoveries which were made in the fifteenth and sixteenth centuries. Ships could be steered using rhumb lines, which were direct courses of constant bearing from one point to another; but it was essential that the master or pilot knew how to correct a course whenever it became necessary.

It was an essential part of a pilot's skill to pick his way through a channel and although the approaches to the channel ports would have been well recorded with plenty of onshore marks, it was still necessary to record the depth of the water and the nature of the sea-bed. **Lead weights** or **sounds** were used to measure the depth of water beneath the ship. Each had a small recess in its base which could be filled with tallow to enable the leadsman to 'sample' the sea-bed as well as measure the depth of the water.

A log reel found on the upper deck in the after castle
This was used with a line and a chip to measure the distance a ship travelled within a certain time span. The line was calibrated with knots, and the number of knots on the line paid out to keep the chip in the same position as the ship moved forward, were counted during a period of time measured by a sand glass. Captain John Smith writing in 1627 said 'that it [the log line] is so uncertain, it is not worth the labour to try it' but the method remained in use for over two centuries.

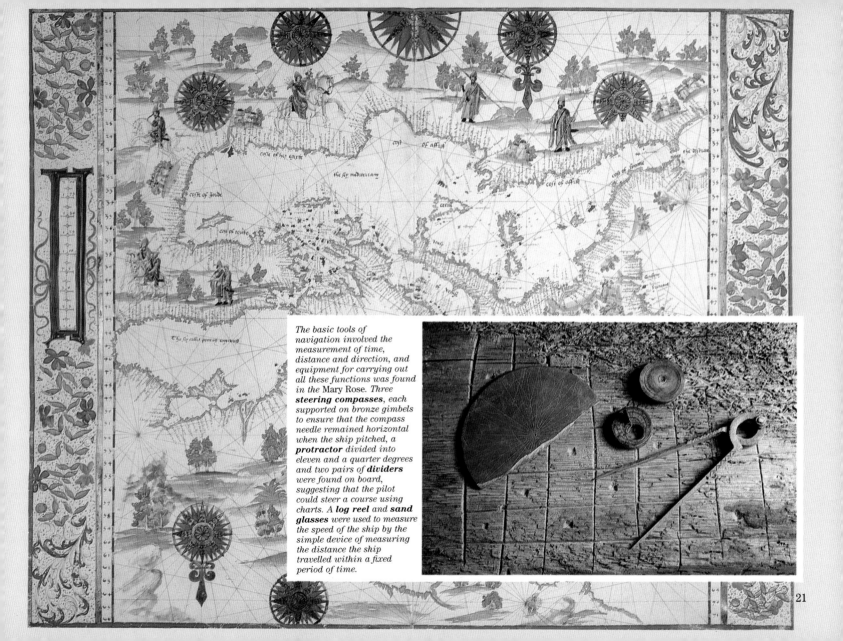

The basic tools of navigation involved the measurement of time, distance and direction, and equipment for carrying out all these functions was found in the Mary Rose. Three **steering compasses**, each supported on bronze gimbels to ensure that the compass needle remained horizontal when the ship pitched, a **protractor** divided into eleven and a quarter degrees and two pairs of **dividers** were found on board, suggesting that the pilot could steer a course using charts. A **log reel** and **sand glasses** were used to measure the speed of the ship by the simple device of measuring the distance the ship travelled within a fixed period of time.

Guns and Munitions of War

The technological advances made in the manufacture of guns for use on land or at sea in the first half of the sixteenth century are reflected in the ordnance recovered from the *Mary Rose*.

The inventory of the *Mary Rose* includes two main types of gun in addition to hand guns: **breech-loading** and **muzzle-loading**. The larger **wrought iron guns** were mounted on wooden beds or stocks which could be moved on a pair of wheels supported on a single axle. These guns were breech-loading, each equipped with several chambers which held the powder charge, so there was no need to withdraw the gun from the port in order to reload it with either shot or powder.

Guns of this type had been in use for two centuries with only minor technical improvements but Henry VIII actively encouraged the development of a gun founding industry and some of the earliest **cast bronze guns** made in London for King Henry were also recovered from the *Mary Rose*.

These new bronze weapons were muzzle-loading and they were fitted to elm carriages which enabled them to be run back for cleaning and reloading. They fired iron shot which could damage either the rigging or the light superstructure of an enemy ship and, according to Sherrif in 1590,

some of them would have had a point blank range of 340 to 400 paces or a random range of 1,700 to 2,500 paces.

Used within the confines of the gun ports on the main deck, it was impossible to manoeuvre the guns with any accuracy. Instead the guns were fired as the ship moved and brought them to bear on the enemy.

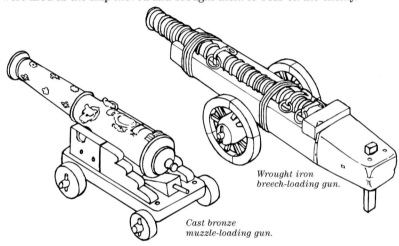

Wrought iron breech-loading gun.

Cast bronze muzzle-loading gun.

From the Anthony Inventory of 1546

Guns of Brass		Guns of Iron		Shot of Iron		Shot of Stone and Lead	
Cannon	2	Portpieces	12	For Cannon	50	For Portpieces	200
Demi Cannon	2	Slings	2	For Demi Cannon	60	For Fowlers	170
Culverins	2	Demi Slings	3	For Culverins	60	For Top Pieces	20
Demi Culverins	6	Quarter Slings	1	For Demi Culverins	140	For Bases	400
Sakers	2	Fowlers	6	For Sakers	80	For Hand Guns	1,000
Falcons	1	Bases	30	For Falcons	60		
		Top Pieces	2	For Slings	40		
		Hailshot	20	For Demi Slings	40		
		Hand Guns	50	For Quarter Slings	50		
				Dice or Iron			

Rapid repeat firing was impossible, but used in conjunction with the wrought iron guns, which could be loaded with either iron 'anti-ship' shot or stone 'anti-personnel' shot, this provided a well-balanced battery of ordnance.

The efficiency of the iron guns at long range is open to question. Certainly at short range they would have been effective, their stone shot shattering on impact would have had a devastating effect on both personnel and rigging. As breech-loaders, they could be rapidly re-loaded with charged powder chambers without having to move the gun itself. Bronze guns would be used at distance and the iron guns at close quarters, affording an integrated weapons system.

Greater flexibility was provided by the smaller breech-loading **swivel guns** which were rapid fire weapons. They were mounted on stirrups in sockets cut into the rails or into the sills of small ports high in the fore and after castles. A tail-like tiller extended behind the breech and this enabled the gunner to depress, elevate or swivel the gun as required. The swivel guns from the *Mary Rose* vary in size from forty-six to sixty-five millimetre bore, and all the complete loaded guns had a cast lead shot, with an offset iron dice inside, in the breech end of the barrel when recovered.

Most of the breech-loading iron guns, including the swivel guns, were made of a number of staves, or bars, of iron which had been formed into a cylinder around a mandrel. Collars and hoops of wrought iron were heated and slipped over the cylinder. As these cooled, they shrank to form a reinforced tube. These 'built up guns' were made in this manner in an attempt to provide a gas-tight barrel, strong enough to withstand the ignition of powder and expulsion of the shot.

Wooden **shot gauges** and a copper alloy **gunner's rule**, calibrated on one side for iron shot and on the reverse for lead shot, were used to enable the correct shot to be selected for each gun. **Powder scoops** were used to load individual guns with a specific charge of powder, and the copper alloy nozzles of **powder flasks** were also found. These had spring-loaded plates which sealed the base of extended nozzles. After the nozzle had been filled with a charge of powder the spring was released and the base of the nozzle sealed, thus controlling the amount of powder delivered. The body of these flasks had been completely destroyed, but they were almost certainly made of horn and, like the horn lights in the lanterns, they had been destroyed by micro-organisms.

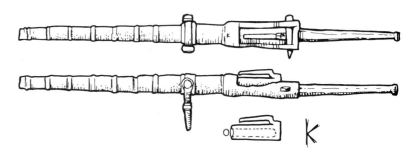

Wrought iron swivel gun or base found beneath the after castle. The separate breech chamber was held in position by an iron wedge and the gun was loaded with lead-covered iron shot weighing 467 grams.

A **linstock** was used to hold the lint, or slow match, which the gunner used to ignite the gun powder in the touch hole of a gun. They were the personal property of individual gunners and many of them had been decorated with chip carving to create the form of a dragon's head which then held the lighted match in its mouth.

Wooden **rams** to pack the charge home and **reamers** or **priming wires** to break open a powder cartridge or clean the touch hole, complete the accessories necessary to fire the large guns. **Tampions** and wads were used to hold the charge in position in the barrel and to seal the open end of a gun or a breech chamber.

The guns were used to bombard enemy ships and strafe the soldiers and gunners as they came within range, but once the ship had closed, it became a matter of hand-to-hand warfare and **pikes, bills, swords** and **daggers** were more useful than the heavy guns. Many staff weapons including pikes and bills were found on the upper deck in the after castle and the close proximity of **boxes of arrows** and **longbows** suggests that ready-to-use equipment was placed here where it was easily accessible.

As Jean Froissart, the fourteenth-century French historian, observed 'Battles at sea are more dangerous and fiercer than battles on land: for on the sea there is no recoiling or fleeing; there is no remedy but to fight and to abide fortune, and every man to show his prowess.' For the men on board the *Mary Rose* when she sank there was no recoiling or fleeing. Soldiers and gunners were trapped at action stations, either between decks or beneath the heavy netting which covered the joists above the upper deck in the waist of the ship.

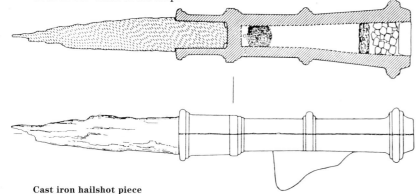

Cast iron hailshot piece

Three small, cast iron guns were found on the upper decks in the after castle and one from the fore castle. They were all muzzle-loading weapons with a rectangular bore, loaded with powder, wad and iron cubes or dice. Beneath each gun there was a projecting hook which was used to hold the gun in position over a rail and a wooden stock or tiller at the rear helped the gunner direct his charge at the enemy. These guns were light and portable and they could be used to repel boarders at close range. Twenty hailshot pieces of this type were listed in the ship's inventory.

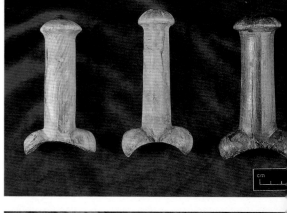

Three of the sixty-four kidney dagger handles, the majority made of boxwood, recovered from the Mary Rose. *This is the largest typological and dateable group of kidney daggers or ballock-knives from a single source in existence.*

Careful excavation on the upper deck of the ship revealed the shape of what at first appeared to be a complete sword. However, all that remained was a 'shadow' caused by the corroding steel staining the surrounding sediment.

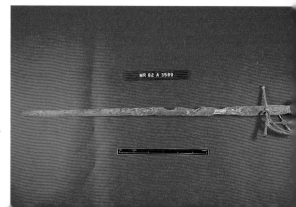

Although the wooden handles of thirty-four swords were recovered, only one almost complete example was found. Trapped beneath the after castle at the stern of the ship, the sword survived deeply buried in an environment almost devoid of oxygen.

Internal view of a section of the main and upper deck reconstructed to full scale in the Mary Rose Museum. The bronze and iron guns on the main deck are the original ones which were found protruding through the open gun ports when the ship was excavated. The light colour planking and blinds, which provided protection for the gunners and archers on the upper deck, are made from poplar, unlike the main hull which is oak. Poplar was less likely to splinter if it was shattered by enemy gun fire.

Alternate blinds could be removed if necessary to provide a port for an archer or gunner.

The gun port lids were made of four planks fastened together with iron bolts. The inner vertical planks were cut slightly smaller than the outer horizontal planks to provide a waterproof rebate when the lid was shut.

The Archery Equipment

The longbow was the supreme weapon of war in medieval times but by the middle of the sixteenth century it was being superseded by the handgun.

Most of the inventories of weapons on board the King's ships include longbows and arrows and it is clear, from the excavation evidence, that fully-equipped archers were alongside gunners when the *Mary Rose* sank.

More than **3,500 arrows** and **137 whole longbows** were recovered from the ship. Some were with the archers at action stations on the upper decks, but many were in closed boxes in the storage area on the orlop deck or stowed, ready-to-use, in boxes on the upper deck in the after castle.

Several of the archers were equipped with **sheaves** of 24 arrows spaced within a leather disc. Stitch marks around the edge of the disc indicate that a fabric sleeve had been attached to the disc to protect the shafts.

As all the stitch marks were on the lower edge of the disc it appears that the sleeve was single ended, and protected the lower ends of the shafts only. There would have been a drawstring at the lower end to enable the archer to withdraw an arrow by pulling it downwards through the leather disc and out of the sleeve.

Many of the arrow shafts were of poplar, but shafts of beech, ash and hazel were also found. Draw lengths of arrows varied between 61 and 81 centimetres with the majority having a draw length of 76 centimetres. Only minute fragments of the feather flights remained, identified as goose or swan. None of the steel tips have survived. All of the arrows had a notch for the bowstring, reinforced with a small sliver of horn inserted at right angles to it.

The bow staves recovered from the *Mary Rose* were made from a single baulk of wood cut from the trunk of a yew tree. After careful seasoning it was cleft radially into a series of triangular billets. The bowyer was careful to retain the sapwood layer, which occurs between the dense heartwood and the bark of the tree, to preserve the natural laminate of two 'types' of wood with quite different properties; the heartwood, which faced the archer,

One box of longbows was raised intact and investigated on the deck of the diving vessel Sleipner. *No horn nocks were found inside, nor, as with the other bows recovered, was there any evidence for binding on the grip. Careful examination revealed that many bows were marked with one of a series of impressed 'pock' marks to signify the position where the arrow should be placed when the bow was drawn.*

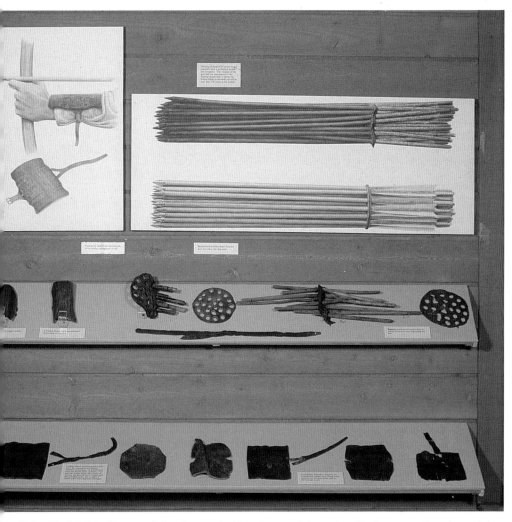

performing better under compression and the sapwood better under tension.

The staves were shaped to a D-section with a flat back of sapwood and a rounded belly of heartwood. Tillering notches were cut on opposite sides of the bow at each end enabling the bow to be braced and the upper and lower limbs to be shaped.

A horn nock was then fashioned to fit each tip and the bows were strung ready to brace the bow and shoot the arrow. No trace of bowstrings could be found, even among the barrels stored in the hold. While their position on the ends of the bows was clearly indicated by the presence of lighter coloured and less degraded wood in these areas, all but one of the horn nocks had disappeared.

The average length of the bows is 1·98 metres (range 1·87 to 2·11 metres). The average height of the men was 1·72 metres but some of the men associated with archery equipment were 1·83 metres tall.

Left: *Arrow spacers and wristguards.*

Right: *(Top) Original horn nock, found encased within the corroded remains of body armour, the only surviving example of the hundreds which would have been on board the ship. (Middle) The lighter coloured wood at the tip of this longbow gives a clear indication of a nocks position. (Bottom) This longbow is fitted with a replica nock to show how the finished article would have looked.*

Life on Board

The crew of the *Mary Rose* in 1545 as listed in the Anthony Roll was 200 mariners, 185 soldiers and 30 gunners, although one account says that there were 700 men on board when she sank. At best, men lived, worked, and fought in cramped, overcrowded conditions, but their rate of pay compared well with farmworkers and craftsmen ashore. Food, clothing and essential equipment were provided for their use, and in January 1545 the wages of a mariner were raised from 5*s.* to 6*s.* 8*d.* a month (one third of £1) – the equivalent of one day's pay for an Admiral. Only the names of the Vice Admiral, Sir George Carew and the Captain, Roger Grenville are known, but a study of the crew's belongings and their physical remains confirms that they were a group of relatively young, robust men who ate reasonably well, dressed with some comfort and elegance and entertained themselves in their off-watch periods. Sweet-smelling laurel leaves helped to freshen the foul air between decks and a small pewter 'piss pot' and pomander, which may have held herbs and spices, shows that at least one officer made special provision for his own comfort. Unfortunately, the loss of the castle at the bow and much of the after castle means that no evidence of the 'heads' or latrines has survived.

Relatively few pottery or glass vessels were found on board with the understandable exception of the barber surgeon's equipment.

Fine **pewter dishes, plates, tankards** and **spoons** provided elegant and hard-wearing tableware for the officers; while the soldiers and sailors generally used **wooden bowls, dishes, plates** and **stave-built tankards**. A barrel of **tallow candles** was found in the stores on the orlop deck and **candleholders** of pewter, brass and wood were also found. The use of candlesticks created a serious fire hazard and their use was strictly limited. Only the dim light of candle-lit **lanthorns** (lanterns), with sheets of horn instead of glass, were available to light the ship at night.

The remains of some two hundred individuals found on board the ship have been studied. They fall into four main age ranges, with most of the individuals being in their late teens or early twenties. However, there were a few boys, and some men in their forties.

The average height of the mature adults was 1·72 metres, and they were all healthy young men. Nevertheless, evidence of childhood dietary deficiency is quite common.

In the **galley**, located in the hold just forward of the step for the main mast, was a massive brick-built **oven**. Here, the crew's food was cooked in two large **cauldrons** supported on iron bars over a fire box. Smaller bronze, iron and ceramic **cooking pots** were also found nearby. Fuel for the fire, in the form of quartered, halved or whole **logs** cut to a standard length, was found stacked ready to use in the bay immediately forward of the galley. Close by lay a pair of **bellows** and two wooden **ash-boxes**.

A study of **meat bones,** both cattle and pig, found in casks suggests that animals were selected and butchered to meet standard specifications. The inclusion of marrow bones was avoided, presumably because they would have gone rancid more quickly than other bones.

Backgammon and other dice games were played on board the ship.

Eighteenth-century instructions show that the selection of meat cuts to be stored in casks was of prime importance: 'The beef provided for His Majesty's ships is to be cut into four pound pieces, and the pork into two pound pieces; and no unusual pieces are to be put up such as leg bones, shins of oxen, cheeks of hogs . . .' Similarly, cod of standard size were found in barrels and baskets at the stern of the ship.

In 1565, twenty years after the *Mary Rose* sank, naval victuallers contracted to supply each sailor with the following rations per week:

7 pounds biscuits	¾ pound stock fish
7 gallons beer	⅜ pound butter
8 pounds salt beef	¾ pound cheese

The **silts** which filled the hull of the *Mary Rose* soon after she sank have preserved many minute clues to life on board as well as evidence which will help us understand the processes of colonisation, partial destruction and final preservation, which began as soon as the ship sank to the sea-bed. Small **oyster shells** which settled as spat on the bronze guns and inside the open gun ports were smothered and killed within eighteen months, whereas others on the outside of the after castle grew to full maturity before they dropped off the collapsing structure. Fine, clean light-coloured silts deposited over organic remains within the hull, provided an **anaerobic atmosphere** which prevented the growth of most bacteria, moulds and fungi and ensured the preservation of silk, wool, wood and leather. At the same time, steel, horn and linen objects have been almost totally destroyed.

At an early stage of the excavation a decision was made to sample all the silts within the ship in the hope that evidence of the microfauna which must have existed on board might be preserved. Over 2,000 samples were taken and the study of insect, botanical and mammalian material preserved in those samples continues. Insect remains, seeds and grasses all provide evidence for life on board. The bones of an immature **rat**, possibly the black rat, and a small **dog** were found in addition to the meat and fish bones derived from food in casks. The presence of **broom** twigs and pods reminds us that broom was often burnt on board ships to fumigate them. **Peppercorns** were found in seamen's chests and in a turned wooden canister in the barber surgeon's cabin. They were used to relieve flatulence as well as providing flavouring for the often-monotonous meals.

Seeds including agrimony, caught up in woollen clothing, and **plum stones** have been indentified as well as various 'straws' and grasses.

1 **Samples of fish bones**
 Some of the fish bones, including conger eel, found trapped beneath an oak barrel on the orlop deck.
2 **Sampling within the hull**
 Samples of silt trapped behind the ceiling planking in the hold contain environmental evidence including insect remains and wood chippings which probably derived from when the ship was built or repaired.
3 **Sample of peppercorns**
 From the barber surgeon's cabin.

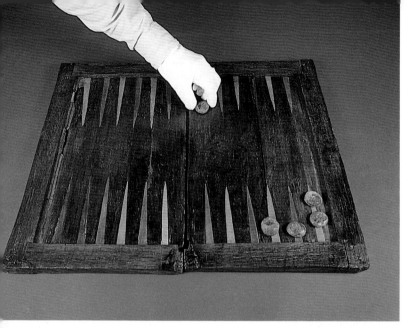

In their spare time the crew relaxed with books, music and games. The most elaborate gaming board was a fine **backgammon set** made of oak with spruce and yew inlays. This was found folded and closed, complete with its counters, in a cabin used by the ship's carpenter. **Merrills**, or nine men's morris, and what is probably a crude **backgammon board** were found scratched into the end of a small barrel. Eleven dice, made of bone, were also discovered among personal possessions stored in chests and leather pouches. Gaming at tables was popular in the Tudor period and high stakes were often involved.

Three tabor **pipes** and a **tabor**, or drum, were found in the crew's quarters abaft the main mast and among the personal chests stored on the orlop deck. The musician would play the pipe and drum in the style of a one-man band: playing the melody on the pipe while beating the rhythm on the drum with the other hand. Fragments of two **fiddles** were also recovered. However without doubt the finest musical instrument is a **shawm**, found carefully stored inside a stave-built case. More properly known as a douçaine or still shawm, this sophisticated instrument is unique. The normal loud shawm, an early form of oboe, is well documented. But, prior to its discovery, the only clue to the still shawm having existed came from obscure written references. With an extra hole for the thumb, it had a musical range more like a clarinet and could produce a quieter sound, rather than the loud, piercing noise usually associated with such instruments.

Nothing is known about the musicians themselves. But the presence of shawm reminds us that it was not unusual in Queen Elizabeth I's time for senior officers to have professional musicians with them on board ship, and the same may have happened in her father's time. Certainly the fact that the instruments found on the *Mary Rose* were tuned so they could be played together, suggests that there was a band on board.

Some of the men were literate. Leather **book covers** survive, although the paper pages have long since disappeared. **Quill pens** and **ink pots** were also found, and the archives contain letters written on board the *Mary Rose* by her various commanders. However not everyone could read, and objects were marked with distinctive graffiti and brands to denote ownership. Significant areas of the ship were also clearly marked, including essential items like hatches and hatch covers to show which cover fitted which hatch. Similarly the chambers of breech-loading guns usually had the same mark as the gun they fitted. Such easily recognisable identifying marks were essential if the ship was to function safely and efficiently.

Above: *Backgammon board.*
Below: *Musical instruments.*

Make and Mend

Many objects were made, repaired or modified while the ship was at sea.

A **bag of leather shoes** awaiting repair and a sole of a shoe cut out of the side of an old leather bucket indicate that help was on hand to repair old shoes and make new ones out of old materials. **Ribbon, braid, thread, buttons, pins**, and **thimbles** were also found, and some of the clothes have neatly darned tears and patches.

Stone **shot moulds** and roughly cut strips of lead indicate that some shot were cast on board, but more surprising was the discovery of an **unfinished shot mould** showing that the moulds were either made or finished on board ship. Large **unfinished stone shot** were also found with grooves cut into the roughly cut lump of stone so that it could be held firmly in a noose while it was finished with a hammer and chisel. An **unfinished linstock** and a rejected, inaccurately cut moulding plane are two other objects which were made by the individual owner or tradesman as he needed them.

Many personal objects including linstocks, which held the gunner's 'lint' or match with which he fired the gun, and wooden knife sheaths were also found with enthusiastic chip carving or incised decoration.

Mary Rose carpentry items including: mallet, brace, various planes, rulers, mortise gauge and whetstone. In the foreground is a selection of nails.

Above: *The large **grindstone** found on the orlop deck at the bow was supported in a heavy wooden block and its main use was for sharpening tools and knives. The iron spindle on which it rotated was almost completely corroded away; it was probably turned by hand rather than by a foot treadle.*

Below: *One of the earliest examples of a **weaving tool** for use at sea was found in a cabin on the main deck in the fore castle. This loom was crudely carved from oak, with a roughly shaped handle at the head end. Well used, it had been repaired with a wooden batten across the base, which covered and strengthened a cracked area between two of the slats.*

The loom would have been strung with a continuous line which passed alternately through the holes and slots in the loom and around two battens, one of which was secured to a back-strap which passed around the weaver's waist. The line connecting the loom with the battens formed the warp. By raising and lowering the loom, the line passing through the holes and the line passing through the slots could be raised and lowered alternately. The weaving line, or weft, could then be passed between the upper and lower warp. A small wooden knife, known in the Royal Navy as a 'sword', was used to push the weft to the end of the riband. A second batten at the weaver's waist acted as a 'brake' to hold the finished work.

Its main use was to make strops, for lifting equipment and stores, and ribbon-like mats to protect and bind areas of rigging which were subjected to heavy wear.

The earliest reference to a loom of this type at sea comes from a Swedish treatise on rigging written in 1691, but a similar tool was found on the Armada vessel La Trinidad Valencera *which was wrecked off the coast of the Republic of Ireland in 1588.*

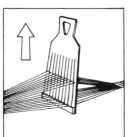

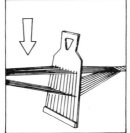

The Barber Surgeon

Any serious spread of infection among the closely packed community in the ship would make it impossible to man the ship effectively and for this reason a surgeon and his mate were normally included in the crew. These men were often highly skilled and Robert Symson who was Master Surgeon on board the *Mary Rose* in 1513 became second warden of the Company of Barber Surgeons in 1526. In 1540, an Act of Parliament formalised the union of the Fellowship of Surgeons with the Barbers' Company and Henry VIII presented a charter to the Guild of Barber Surgeons in that year.

We do not know the name of the barber surgeon on board the ship when she sank, but the remains of his cabin were found on the starboard side of the main deck close to the guns and the soldiers at action stations. Working in these cramped conditions with only 1·6 metres headroom below the deck beams the surgeon had, to act as apothecary and physician as well as barber and surgeon. It is doubtful if he ever undertook extensive surgery, but he would have been able to amputate a wounded limb and cauterise wounds to promote healing. The cabin was sparsely furnished with a large **wooden chest** and a **four-legged bench** for preparing plasters or dressings. Inside the chest were sixty-four objects, including nine **wooden-lidded canisters** containing **ointments** and a similar one containing **peppercorns**. Nicholas Culpeper's herbal, 'The English Physition' published in l652, specifies the use of pepper for agues and quinsy; while in 1617 John Woodall, the first Surgeon General of the East India Company, had described the use of black pepper to expel wind! Two metal **syringes** for urethral injections, the handles of **surgical tools** and a **bleeding-bowl** were also recovered. **Razors,** a **whetstone** and a **shaving-bowl** completed the barber surgeon's kit.

Working on board a ship within a limited community, the surgeon had ample opportunity to observe the transmission of disease from one man to another, and Woodall recognised the need for good hygiene and recommended the use of clean 'pipes' for each patient treated with the urethral syringe.

The box also contained medicines in **five corked jars** which had been made in Raeren in Germany and may have been imported as medicinal

containers, as well as several ready to use rolls of ointment, kept close to hand to treat wounds without delay.

Pewter plates, canisters and **flasks** were found strewn around the box together with a **chafing-dish** for warming medicine. A large **apothecary's mortar** and **drug containers** in pewter, glass and wood lay among more personal possessions such as a purse of silver coins, leather shoes and wooden combs.

The location of the cabin, close to action stations on the main gun deck, indicates the need for the surgeon to be close at hand when the ship was engaged for battle. While surgery was limited, indeed brutal, if our surgeon followed Woodall's later instructions, to 'daily visit the men to see who hath any sickness or imperfection', the men on the *Mary Rose* were better cared for than their contemporaries ashore.

Clothing

Personal items, such as clothing and food utensils were sometimes purchased on behalf of the King and issued to the soldiers and mariners on board his ships; the accounts of the royal wardrobe contain references to the purchase of 'coats of green and white' (the Tudor colours) for the use of soldiers on board the *Mary Rose* at a cost of 34 pence (6s. 10d.) each in 1511. These 'uniforms' may have been intended purely for ceremonial use and none was found on board the ship when she was excavated. However, turned wooden bowls and stave-built wooden tankards were found marked with a crudely incised arrow to denote that they were paid for from the royal wardrobe accounts.

Deeply buried in the silts, knitted and woven wool, silk and leather survived well within the wreck, while garments of linen and objects of horn have almost entirely disappeared. Therefore, while we have a fine assemblage of **leather shoes** and **jerkins** and fragments of **worsted** and **knitted garments**, we have no information about the undergarments or the breeches which were almost certainly made of linen.

Satin covered buttons, silk embroidered purses and **fine lace** trimmings hint at the elegant clothing worn by some of the officers and many of the leather jerkins are fashionably cut and beautifully finished. Two almost complete **caps**, each with a single brim worked as a hem, had been knitted in stocking stitch and then felted, brushed and fitted with a silk lining.

Another knitted item, probably a **scogger** – a type of footless legging or detachable sleeve, had been knitted on four needles and fashioned into a funnel shape by decreasing one stitch at the end of each needle at eighteen to twenty millimetre intervals. Knitted sleeves were mentioned in an Act of Parliament in 1552 and they would have been useful additional protection for a sailor in cold weather.

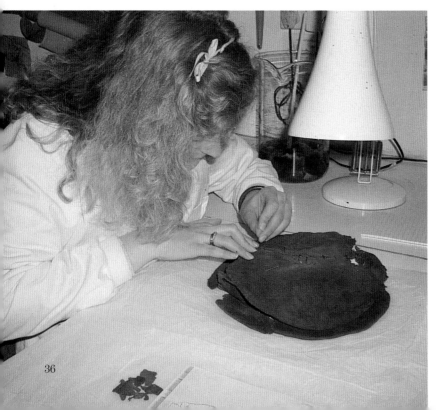

Left: *Conservator prepares cap for display.*

Right: *As much a badge of office as headdress, this hat of silk velvet was found in the Barber Surgeon's cabin.*

Twelve leather jerkins have been reconstructed and studied in detail. All were made in oak tanned calfskin and three main types have been identified:
  (i) with centre front fastening;
 (ii) with side fastening;
(iii) with crossover front.

These garments were fashioned to fit the man's body as well as his taste in fashion and they provide additional evidence about his physique and help us to understand his muscular development. Many are decorated with pinking and slashing and one is elaborately finished with bound edges, stand-up collar and a pocket inside the 'skirt' on the left-hand side. The armholes were finished with a decorative roll of leather which was piped and slashed.

Fragments of clothing made from woven woollen cloth have been conserved, but only two items have been studied in sufficient detail to attempt a reconstruction of the whole garment. Some of the more interesting fragments are the remains of a pair of woollen knee-length hose. They were worn with a pair of flat-soled shoes with a narrow strap which fastened over the instep. All these clothes were personal possessions of individuals and, like the fashionable shoes and boots which many of the men wore, they provide a rare insight into everyday fashion in the middle of the sixteenth century.

Every fragment of clothing is drawn and recorded in detail before it is conserved, and from these drawings accurate polythene patterns can be made of each individual piece. After conservation it is sometimes possible to add further detail of stitch marks or thread impressions. These polythene patterns are invaluable guides in understanding how the garments were constructed – seams can be matched and binding pieces and gussets correctly positioned by juggling the jigsaw puzzle of polythene scraps. Once the garment pieces fit together, a felt copy can be made and from this we get our first estimation of the stature of the man who wore it.

Finally, leather or wool replicas can be made for display and study. The fragile leather fragments remain preserved in a carefully controlled environment for further study by specialists if necessary in the future.

Above: *Studying jerkin.*   **Below:** *Leather shoes.*

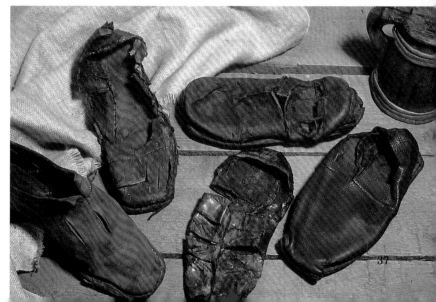

Many of our objects are the earliest dated example and, if found in isolation, would have been ascribed to a later date.

The *Mary Rose* serves to remind us that this was the Renaissance, when art and science blossomed, and when the King hired the best he could, to cast his guns and build his ships.